GASES

by Robin Nelson

first step nonfiction

⌐ Lerner Publications Company · Minneapolis

We live on Earth.

Earth is made of
different things.

Earth is made of rocks, soil,
water, and gases.

A **gas** is something that can change shape and size.

It is not a **solid.**

It is not a **liquid.**

Gases float around Earth.

Gases **protect** Earth.

Air is a gas that
people breathe.

Air takes up space.

We can't see air.

We can feel air when the
wind blows.

Steam is a gas.

Steam is hot water that has
turned into a gas.

Gases are all around us.

Gases are found on Earth.

Air Pollution

Air is made of different gases. Sometimes dirt and chemicals get into the air. This is called pollution. Most pollution comes from things people do, like drive cars and make electricity. Air pollution can make it hard for animals and people to breathe. What can we do to stop air pollution?

Great Gas Facts

 Gases trap the heat from the sun in the air. This warms our planet.

 Volcanoes shoot gases and rock out when they explode. These gases cause natural air pollution.

 Gases always fill their container no matter what shape. If you squeeze a balloon, the gas moves to fill the balloon's new shape.

Gases that start as liquids are called vapor. Clouds are made of water vapor.

 Helium is a gas that is lighter than air. It is used to make balloons float.

 Neon gas can glow. Many stores have neon signs.

 Gases are always moving. When a gas with an odor is released in a room, you can smell it in all parts of the room very quickly.

Glossary

 gas – something that fills up whatever space it is in

 liquid – something that you can pour

 protect – to keep safe

 solid - something that has a definite shape

 steam – water that has become a gas

Index

The photographs in this book are reproduced through the courtesy of: © Ludovic Maisant/ CORBIS, cover, p. 14; © Royalty-Free/CORBIS, pp. 2, 6, 7, 13, 22 (second from top), 22 (second from bottom); © Ron Watts/CORBIS, p.3; © W. Cody/CORBIS p. 4; © Buddy Mays/CORBIS pp. 5, 22 (top); © 1996 CORBIS; original image courtesy of NASA/CORBIS, p. 8; © Bettmann/ CORBIS, pp. 9, 22 (middle); © Norbert Schaefer/CORBIS, p. 10; © Richard Hutchings/ CORBIS, p. 11; © Laura Doss/CORBIS, p. 12; © Roy Morsch/CORBIS, pp. 15, 22 (bottom); © Tamara Reynolds/CORBIS, p. 16; © PhotoDisc Royalty Free by Getty Images, p. 17.

Lerner Publications Company
A division of Lerner Publishing Group
241 First Avenue North
Minneapolis, MN 55401 U.S.A.

Website address: www.lernerbooks.com

Library of Congress Cataloging-in-Publication Data

Nelson, Robin, 1971–
    Gases / by Robin Nelson.
        p.   cm. — (First step nonfiction)
    Includes index.
    ISBN: 0–8225–2616–6 (lib. bdg. : alk. paper)
    1. Gases—Juvenile literature. I. Title. II. Series.
QC161.2.N45 2005
533—dc22   2004020786

Manufactured in the United States of America
1 2 3 4 5 6 – DP – 10 09 08 07 06 05